The Pa... lt
A Gre...

Celebrate life daily!!

Paula J. Smith

By Paula J. Smith

First Printing: September 1985
Second Printing: December 1985
Third Printing: March 1986
Fourth Printing: August 1986
Fifth Printing: July 1987
Sixth Printing: September 1988
Seventh Printing: May 1990
Eighth Printing: November 1990
Ninth Printing: July 1991
Tenth Printing: April 1992
Eleventh Printing: October 1992
Twelfth Printing: April 1993
Thirteenth Printing: May 1993
Fourteenth Printing: August 1993
Fifteenth Printing: December 1993
Sixteenth Printing: April 1994
ISBN: 0-914749-01-3
Printed in the United States of America

Printed by: Progress Press, Inc.
                 2922 Nicholas Ave., N.E.
                 Roanoke, VA 24012

Published by: RiskTrek Company
                 Serenity's Edge
                 Route 1, Box 558
                 Thaxton, VA 24174, U.S.A.
                 (703) 947-2468

To my family,

With whom I most wanted to share these thoughts.

ACKNOWLEDGMENTS

My deepest appreciation goes to the following people:

Mary Armentrout, editor, whose faith and enthusiasm for my work kept me going, for all her fine editing; Sarah Reid, Annette Overstreet and Betty Curry, close friends who gave so much of their time in discussing the concept of this book; Rich Friedel, for assistance in putting these ideas into print; Kurt Smith, my husband, whose support was of great comfort!

TABLE OF CONTENTS

The quilt pattern used throughout the book is from a fabric called "Natural Charm" manufactured by Spring Mills, Inc.

THE PATCH-WORD QUILT: A GREAT COMFORTER!

Introduction and purpose:

A patchwork comforter is made up of many different fabric scraps gathered from numerous sources. The scraps are usually collected over a period of time until enough are saved to make a quilt top. When sewn together, you will see that though some of the fabric patterns may clash with one another, they blend together beautifully as a whole.

What makes a patchwork quilt fun to assemble is that you never know how it will turn out. No two patchwork quilts are ever the same. Each quilt top reflects changes in your taste of clothes and in your available fabric sources at that time in your life. The results are always colorful and pleasing to the eye, as well as providing you a practical, warm comforter. And, it becomes a permanent statement of your unique life's history.

When my husband and I were newlyweds, we frequently went on camping trips. It was a cheap and satisfying way of entertaining and enjoying ourselves. At the time, we did not own any sleeping bags. Instead, we'd pile up a bunch of patchwork quilts I'd made to fight off the frigid 20-degree nights. We were indeed, snug as a bug in a rug!

Though frayed and worn a bit today, they continue to provide us with warmth and comfort. They seem appropriate and natural to have and to use wherever we are or go. These are the "work horses" of the quilt family. They weren't designed to be carefully and delicately placed on a sofa back, providing that ornamental look. They were made to be used! Yet, at the same time, they serve as a constant reminder of that simpler, less complicated, old-fashioned way of life. With the pace of our lives ever increasing, zooming by so rapidly, appearing more and more complicated, our old patchwork quilts seem to reach out and tell us to slow down and relax—something my husband and I have found difficult to do!

Thus, it seems appropriate to use the patch-work quilt as the symbol and theme for this little book. The words are not new. They've been around for centuries. It's perhaps, an odd and unusual collection of words bound together by the fact that they all involve RISK.

Risk-taking touches every area of your life. It's a vast entity that encompasses all from the simplest things to the very complex. Everything you do in your life involves a certain amount of risk.

Life involves a constant process of change. Change is the one thing in life you can count on to be constant! So, the risks you face will always be changing, too.

The contents of this book evolved over a period of time in my own life, when I was fighting my own set of stresses and felt **very** desperate. I found comfort in writing down my thoughts and re-reading them from time to time. I still have problems and crises in my life—always will. But I've discovered that it helps to settle down and quietly reflect on a

3

regular basis. After doing this, I usually find that I'm calmer, more accepting and comfortable with being me. I am then able to handle what I am capable of handling and am also willing to leave the rest to God.

In these fast-moving times, there is a tendency to feel isolated, lonely, and alienated from others or even yourself. These are the times when you need to be surrounded by a little extra warmth and reassurance. This patchwork of words provides something to wrap yourself up in for a few moments, to warm and reassure your cold heart. It's there to comfort you when your negative thoughts and problems have you shuddering and shivering.

The format of this book is in alphabetical order. You can easily and quickly find the ideal or word which you wish to study, work on or just think about.

Use it on a daily basis. Key in on one word and repeat it throughout the day—remembering the thoughts you read. This will help you

4

remain conscious of the way you are—where you are now versus your ideal. Be aware, and be motivated by your desire to change, and positive things **will** begin to happen.

This is a working book. It does no good if placed on your bookshelf. It's small so that you can carry it with you wherever you go. The purpose of this book is to help you focus, to bring clarity, comfort and assurance, and offer strength when you need it. You will never need to feel that you're alone—much comfort lies between these two covers!

Acceptance means seeing reality for what it is and living in the now. It means having the courage to look at yourself honestly and objectively. It means giving up all the facades and ideals you have that are no longer valid in your life. It requires accepting yourself as you are now.

Only by accepting the situation, yourself, or the other person can you decide what you can do about them. This is fundamental to any self-growth. To ignore or to resist acceptance can often result in personal anguish. If you ignore or resist a problem, it usually continues to grow, becoming more complex. When finally you **do** decide to accept the situation, it is much harder to do so. It requires more effort and more energy to rid yourself of negative factors or your emotional pain.

Acceptance is a slow process. It cannot be hurried or demanded at will. You should not be too harsh on yourself when you are unable to accept circumstances that trouble you—

even though you wish you could. You at least know that you are trying which, in itself, provides some comfort.

Life is an assortment of many pleasant and unpleasant experiences. Acceptance of this, gives you the strength to know that the unpleasant times will soon pass. Because of the tendency to always want more than you have now, you need to stop and look at what you presently have and accept its goodness.

Only when you can truly accept yourself for what you are, can you then accept others wholeheartedly and lovingly for who they are. You cannot change others. You have no power to change them. You have only the power to accept the responsibility to change yourself. By accepting others for what they are and who they are, you will no longer find it necessary to blame, find fault or to demand that others conform to your standards.

Acceptance gives you the key to RISK. It unlocks the door to inner freedom and peace of mind!

Giving of one's self does not include giving advice. Learn to listen instead. When you are really listening, you forget about yourself—and your opinions. You can best give to others by letting them have your complete attention.

Many times other people simply need to know that you truly care. They need you to act as a sounding board. They may ask for your opinions, but by your silence, you help them to find the answers they seek. You force them to listen to what they, themselves, are actually saying. By allowing them to speak their thoughts and feelings out loud, often they will actually "hear" themselves for the first time.

The majority of people do not like receiving advice from others, that they have not requested. Yet how many times do you freely give it? It is best not to answer even when asked. For, who are you that you know all the answers! What is good for one person, may not be good for another.

You can share your life experiences with others but you cannot show them the way out of their problems. The best thing you can do is offer support, understanding and acceptance. You can offer hope by encouraging the person to look within him or herself for solutions. Deep down inside, each of us knows what is best for us. You cannot work out another's problem no matter how badly you want to help. In fact, to tamper, or to try to solve or protect another from his or her problems, can actually make the situation worse.

You have the strength to take the action needed to make changes in your life. That choice and decision can only come from yourself. The answer will not be found in books or through advice received from others, though there are times when seeking God's comfort may aid you in your decision making. You will RISK acting on your problem when, and only when you are ready—having come to your own conclusions as to what is best for you at that moment. Only then will you have true peace. To act on your decisions lets you take responsibility for yourself. You are then taking your own advice!

9

Aloneness does not mean loneliness. It means solitude. There are times when you need solitude. Some need more solitude than others.

Aloneness is necessary for getting in touch with yourself. It's a time when you can take an honest look at yourself without fear of what others will see or think. This is the time to learn how to be your own best friend—when you must confront that inner self that solitude prompts. To accept and enjoy yourself as you are now. To enjoy **being**, for your own sake, is a hard lesson is master. But it is a very rewarding one.

Aloneness becomes a problem if you seek it to the point of purposefully avoiding contact with others. If you see this in yourself, you should be aware of it and start forcing yourself to mix with others. Can you truly survive without the company of others? Or, would you really want to?

One of the nicest things I've ever learned to do for myself is to salute and greet myself several times each day. It's like greeting an old, favorite friend you haven't seen for a long time. I've found myself sipping a cup of coffee and silently saying, "Cheers, P.J.!" It's an instant, simple way of recognizing myself as a person who should be cheered on by herself!

There's a tendency to avoid aloneness, especially at times when you must do those things for yourself that no one else can do for you. In fact, to have others around is almost a hindrance to you. Having others constantly present gives you an "excuse" not to do what needs to be done.

Aloneness is sought through many ways. It may be enjoying the quietness of a church sanctuary, spreading out on a rock next to a gurgling creek, sitting in a grassy field, studying a painting in an art museum, being at a library, or some similar revelry.

Times of aloneness help to rekindle the spirit. These special times give you a chance to touch base with yourself again. Ideally, it would be wise to plan time alone, just as you plan your daily work schedule. Don't RISK slighting yourself by not allowing enough time devoted to just you!

ANGER

W hen you feel angry, it's a clue that something is wrong. Something needs to be placed in the open and examined. To keep it inside is to deliberately poison yourself. Acknowledging anger and yet choosing to do nothing about it means that you are resisting change. It means you are unwilling to face something.

Anger inhibits your growth and cripples any positive efforts that you might put forth. Possessing anger is a luxury you cannot afford. Most compulsive habits involved with excessive eating, spending, drinking or smoking, etc., stem from "stuffing" back anger. This is extremely self-destructive.

There are circumstances that occur in your life where you have no control. You should accept these feelings of anger, but it will do no good to lash out. What good does it do to rant and rave? It only shows that you are as out of control as the set of circumstances you find yourself in. The choice is yours to deal with a situation calmly and rationally **or** be temporarily insane and solve nothing. When you are angry, it helps to pause and think before saying anything. That simple silence helps to center your poise and self-control. Acceptance of the situation and dealing with it in "the now"—rationally—is the better way.

You do have the right to—and the need—to tell others of your feelings. Many times you may fear expressing them because they may create tension and friction in your relationships—especially the closest.

How many times have you chosen to remain silent so as not to spoil the "good times". Or have you felt that there is never a "good" time to voice your concerns for fear of "rocking the boat"? To communicate your true feelings often takes much courage as you are vulnerable when opening yourself up to the possibility of rejection. On the other hand, choosing to remain silent is like letting an infected sore fester and giving it no chance to heal. In voicing your concerns, you are operating on the "heart" level—being true to

14

yourself as well as others. Living on this level is the only way to experience true peace from within.

Accumulated anger often leads to hate. It is usually the result of not being able to separate a person's behavior from the actual person. This involves judging and condemning. You cannot afford to do either. How much energy is wasted—and guilt accumulated—in actively destroying someone? Realize that you are also destroying yourself in this process. Hate leaves deep emotional scars with long-range consequences.

You could rid yourself of much anger if you would RISK taking a serious look at yourself. Many times you may be surprised to discover that it is really not another person or situation that "made" you angry but, rather, something within yourself. The root of much anger is often fear or frustration over your lack of control over someone or something. If you desire growth, you must be honest with yourself in finding out what is really hiding behind your angry feelings.

There are times when the best reaction to anger is laughter! Life is often taken too seriously. Stepping back to look at yourself for a moment may reveal just how ridiculously silly your reasoning really is. You may readily see that you have over-reacted to the point of even being pious. Sharing this is showing your humility.

Please, RISK understanding your anger.

ARGUING

To argue for the sake of arguing is a waste of precious time. There is a tendency to try to "out do" or to get even with the other party. No good can come of this. You **do** have the right—and should, talk about your frustrations, concerns or feelings by stating them simply and factually. You **do not** have the right to lash out and take your opponent by surprise. Naturally, his or her first reaction is to counter attack—and thus the argument ensues.

When you argue, you are usually emotionally out of control. You are apt to say things you later regret. Perhaps it's best to remain silent—call a time out—until able to express your concerns in a civil manner.

How many times have you argued to prove that you were "right" and that the other person was "wrong"? What did all this prove in the end? What actually was gained by it? If you were honest with yourself, you'd probably see it shows you had a need to feel superior.

17

And in the process, lost what humbleness you do have. Would it not be better to experience love and compassion than to experience being "right"?

If you heard a tape recording of your argument, how would you feel? The RISK is to let the other person know of your real feelings in an open and quiet manner. Many times the explosive actions are no more than a cover-up of your **fear** to honestly communicate what you feel inside.

ATTITUDE

Your attitude can either help or hurt you. Having the wrong attitude can actually help to create problems.

Your attitude about something is reflected in all that you are and do. It shows in your voice, your body posture, how you react towards others, and your self-confidence.

When you make judgments about others, usually your attitude is "out of kilter". A healthy attitude is a non-judgmental one.

Your present attitude towards life has an immediate effect on what happens to you daily. What you expect out of life is what you get! Thinking negative thoughts brings about negative results. Consequently, thinking positive thoughts brings about positive results or happenings. Accept the fact that only **you** control your attitude and what you think. It can be changed if you wish it so.

Remember that outward actions should be in

compliance with what you feel inside. If your inner attitude is different from your actions, others will be able to sense a falseness about you—no matter how hard you try to cover it up.

If you are frustrated by your negative attitude towards life in general, or towards some specific problem, why not decide to change it? All you have to do is to make the choice to commit to the positive way of life versus the negative. Having decided this, think how you will now act differently and do it! Why not RISK throwing those negative ways out the window? Wouldn't it make you feel better?

BITTERNESS

Your mind cannot tolerate even a minute of bitterness. It is an absolute poison to your system! Being a poison in its purest form, it is extremely quick and effective. It kills any hope of possessing peace of mind instantaneously. Bitterness steals away any positiveness and zest for life you might have, right before your very eyes. The trouble is, unless you're extremely alert, by the time you've discovered you've breathed in its poisonous vapors, it has already invaded your system and swept away your joyous thoughts and love of life. It has, in its gigantic, whirlwind-vapor of gloom, left behind twisted thoughts, devastated feelings, negative ideas—all adding up to a very sad, sad individual. This is a person who is filled-to-the-brim with fear and hatred, instead of reaping joy and happiness.

Bitterness is similar to a magic trick. You **know** the trick you saw was not really magic, but it happened so quickly that your eyes want to believe what they **sensed** they saw. The real trick in life is knowing the secret in blocking out that false sense of reasoning that bitterness seems to give us.

YOU can ill afford to possess even one tiny drop of this potent, harmful drug. Bitterness dulls your mind so quickly that it opens the doors of your mind wide open, allowing all sorts of undesirable thoughts to enter. One by one, they silently troop in, each carrying its own special weapon—such as jealousy, suspiciousness, delicate trigger-point angers—all staring at you with deceiving glances and fire-angry eyes.

How do you become bitter? It may be a result of sensing that some injustice has been done unto you. Perhaps you've been collecting all those petty grievances, carefully tying and bundling them up together, to form a solid mass of "evidence". Maybe it has to do with some unfinished business you need to attend to and resolve. Do you feel bitter because someone else got the job you wanted? Do you feel jealous because someone else is in a better financial position than you? Do you feel hurt because someone has ignored you?

If you find yourself bitter, it is time to take a look inside yourself. Bitterness acts as an indicator that something is wrong with your thinking. The higher degree of bitterness, the stronger the need to change your thoughts. If you choose to ignore your bitterness, it will become worse and more intensified. And, whether you wish to acknowledge it or not, it will eventually destroy you.

Tired of being bitter? Want to do something about it? LET GO OF IT!! Think of all the energy you are wasting by gripping Bitterness so tightly. Let go of it. Let go and live. Choose to live in the present, the now. Do not live in your past. Decide to no longer hold onto your grievances. RISK replacing your bitterness with love!

B laming means looking for a scapegoat for your problems. Realize that blaming means getting nowhere. Rather, seek to examine how your own attitudes have contributed greatly to the problems you have. Blaming is the "easy", cowardly way out. It is easier than admitting that your attitude is faulty and accepting the responsibility to change that. You cannot escape the consequences of your own mistakes. What good does it do for you to place blame on anyone or yourself? Chances are the situation still exists regardless of whether you blame anyone or not. Why not RISK dealing with the situation? By doing so, you will not experience any negative or "bad" feelings, as compared to the way you usually do, when you blame others.

If you find yourself blaming others and situations for the state and/or quality of your life, you're in **big** trouble with a capital B! Sure, there are things that happen to you that are beyond your control and that you cannot anticipate. But, it is how you react and respond to these situations that counts.

Blamers are those who are disliked intensely and often mistrusted. Who wants to associate with such acidy, nasty persons? These are the individuals whose outlook on life is totally negative and hopeless. These are the persons who need your support. To respond positively is to throw them off balance. They are used to being pitied, argued with and despised. But what they really want—as does each of us, is love and understanding. Whether you are dealing with those you know, strangers—or even yourself, treat them kindly, showing them that you value their self-worth. Acknowledge them as worthwhile, unique human beings. Do not RISK getting caught in their negative, self-defeating traps; rather, RISK helping them (and/or yourself) out!

If you allow yourself to give up an old, out-dated idea, a new one will replace it. In order for any change to take place, you must first be open to change as well as admitting there is a reason you need to change. You admit then, that you are not perfect, yet at the same time, accept yourself where you are now.

In making changes, you should not only concentrate on the end result but you should also be involved in the actual day-to-day living process associated with change. Even if you do not feel you have the actual strength at the moment needed to undertake a particular change, just **acting** as though you have that strength is a start. You have then, activated the process by changing your thought patterns about it.

Change means RISKING. It means taking a chance on the fact that you could be disappointed or surprised with the outcome. There is a certain part of change that you cannot anticipate. There is an unknown factor involved. This means you must have the courage to go on, to get out of your "comfort zone", to face feeling uncomfortable with the unknown or the unfamiliarity of new living patterns and/or thoughts. You are RISKING letting go of comfortable ingrained responses or habits.

Realizing you need to make changes in your-self can be painful. However, knowing this and then choosing to do nothing about the situation is even more painful and is doing yourself a great injustice! When you seek changes, you are willing to live peacefully in your inner world, no matter what your future brings or what others think. You are willing to go beyond your present short-term pleasures to obtain long-term ones.

You do not have to wait for the "perfect" time to begin the process of change. It can begin immediately—not next week or tomorrow, but this very second. However, remember that most changes do not occur instantly. They take time and cannot be rushed without injuring the result or the quality. The RISK of changing is yours—if you're willing!

27

COMPASSION

When you are compassionate, you desire to relieve others' suffering, to lend your support or to comfort them. You care about them. You acknowledge them as human beings. You want them to know that they're not alone.

You may tend to reserve your compassionate feelings, using them mainly on those you truly like or know. Sure, you're mildly courteous towards the store clerk, gas station attendant or waitress. But, if any of these people were to provide what you'd consider "poor" service, how would you act? Probably void of compassion and full of bitter or ill-tempered utterings. Suppose the waitress turned out to be a close friend of yours. How differently would you act? Wouldn't you be inclined to overlook her poor service, knowing that she had a lot of problems at home or was having a bad day? Most likely you'd be much more tolerant because she is someone who matters to you.

Why do you tend to hoard your compassionate feelings? Maybe you don't want to seem "too easy" to others. Perhaps you don't want them to think you're "too forward". Or, you don't want them to think that they're as "good" as you.

You seem to feel it's OK to lash out at these strangers since they are just strangers—nobodies. If they're just nobodies then what better way of getting some of your anger and own pent-up feelings out harmlessly? It doesn't matter to you if you hurt their feelings. Sure it does! They're human beings, alive and breathing and full of feelings and problems and frustrations.

Why can't you feel compassion or love even towards a total stranger? You can. You should. You need to. Compassion is the gift of and for giving. It is what the Golden Rule (do unto others as you would have them do unto you) is all about. Compassion is what helps to make your life more wholesome. It encourages patience and shows you that tolerance is a virtue worth developing. It allows you to accept yourself and others as imperfect human beings—which you are!

Compassion for yourself is even more important than compassion for others. Yet many exclude themselves. You may feel others are more important, that their needs are more pressing than your own. But, sometimes the way you treat yourself tends to be the way you treat others. Therefore, you must RISK self-compassion before you can RISK sharing your compassion with others.

How compassionate are you right now? Can you expand these feelings to encompass everyone? Can you overlook imperfections that are present, knowing that you are, naturally, an imperfect human being too? Work on it. It's one of the best things you can do to further your self-growth.

complacency

Complacency is when you feel totally content and so comfortable that you do not seek to change or expand yourself in any way or direction. While this sounds exactly like what you've always been striving for, it can be deceiving.

Complacency quickly erodes your pride and self-motivation, making you lazy and stale. If this state continues unchecked, you will one day wake up and feel nothing. To experience this can be extremely frightening, as suddenly you realize that you have no purpose or meaning in your life.

Too often you clearly see this state in others but not in yourself. You are quick to let them know they are lazy or wrong. Yet you continue in your own state of complacency, now adding feelings of smugness and superiority. You somehow justify or rationalize that this is OK, when in fact these are the very characteristics you find intolerable in others! This blocks out your capacity to be kind or to understand others as well as yourself.

In a sense, you have reached a plateau. Until you are willing to make changes—and/or amends, you are stuck and cannot grow. It's as if you've encountered a fallen tree across the path you're walking. You cannot walk further until you expend some energy and effort to move the tree. As long as you choose to rest, you will remain frozen—in a state of nothingness.

So, while you want to strive towards your "comfort zone", you need to always keep one foot on the path of self-growth. It is when things suddenly become too easy that you need to examine, and keep in mind, what is important enough to you to be used as your life goals. Further, to RISK finding the courage and strength to always work towards these goals—not become complacent! This is insurance against being accidentally blinded by blissful complacency.

COMPULSIVENESS

B eing able to admit that your compulsive-
ness exists is the first step towards living
truly free of it. Your desire to change this
behavior helps give you the strength needed
to overcome it.

As your self-love and the quality of your life
grows, usually you will find that your destructive habits or behaviors tend to become
less intense and less threatening. Someday
you may no longer view them as problems.
When you exchange these nasty habits for
those of self-honesty and love, there is no
longer any room for them to continue to exist.
Nor is there any reason. You learn to care for
yourself as much as you do for others.

Your compulsive actions could be your way of
keeping a self-imposed isolation. Sometimes
it's a way of hiding from yourself. In being
compulsive, you think you are functioning
independently and have no need for people-
when in fact this is when you may need them
the most!

33

If you find yourself stuck when trying to change your compulsive behavior, ask yourself these questions. "Do I really want to change? And if so, how much? How much am I willing to do? How hard am I willing to work? Why am I resisting change? What am I afraid of? Am I behaving like this without even being consciously aware of it? Am I trying to do or to change too much at one time? Am I being realistic in my expectations? What can I do to make me feel better that is not destructive or self-defeating for myself?" Your answers will provide added insight in helping you master your compulsive behavior.

I've been a compulsive eater and overweight most of my life. Whenever I was sad, hurt, angry, lonely or felt emotionally empty, I'd reach for food. I would literally stuff down food to get rid of my negative feelings. It was my way of providing myself with comfort. For many years I was aware of this in myself, but was still unable or unwilling to do something about it.

Usually, you have to feel enough pain, or face

some type of trauma in order to make permanent changes in compulsive behaviors. Even then, you may still choose the "comfort" of these habits. This is because you know how to deal with yourself as you are. You are comfortable in your responses. To give up your compulsive behavior means that you will feel uncomfortable and must face the unknown. How many people do you know who continued to smoke while dying from emphysema, as did my grandfather? Only you can decide to RISK changing your behavior.

In being fat, I wasn't sure how comfortable I'd feel being thin. I wasn't sure I could accept the potential compliments, admiring stares or blatant wolf whistles. Being thin to me meant displaying a gal who had it all together and I didn't feel that I did. Frankly, I was too scared to allow myself to find out. It was obvious that I wasn't hurting enough, wasn't miserable enough and was too scared to "warrant" my changing. In the meantime, being overweight and out of shape was having an ever increasing negative effect on my physical as well as my mental health.

If left unchecked, compulsive habits become worse as time goes on. You tend to want more and more and are satisfied with less. This is frightening because you are rapidly losing control in demanding more and more of yourself—making it harder and harder to stop. Why is this? Perhaps it's because you feel empty inside and you're desperately trying to fill the void. This is an impossible goal, for you're trying to fill it with the wrong sorts of things. You must find the courage to search for love and find your true contemplative or spiritual needs and there will be no more emptiness. To try to fill yourself with anything less is foolish and can even be dangerous to your well-being.

There's a natural tendency to seek immediate comfort and thus give in easily to your compulsive behaviors since they provide instant gratification—even if negative in scope. In a sense, when this happens, you temporarily go "crazy" as you are blinded to the real goals you've set for yourself. You become your own slavemaster—leaning towards self-hate instead of self-love.

True independence involves your willingness to search within yourself. And to give up self-defeating, compulsive habits. It also involves your willingness to RISK reaching out to others in sharing your honest feelings and love—not stuffing them deep down inside!

My bout with compulsive eating began to become more manageable when I started having the guts to share my feelings openly with others—especially my family. Because I found it too painful to confront them face to face, sharing my thoughts through writings helped me. Try to find a healthy release for your own compulsive behaviors.

This is RISKY business. Acknowledging and giving up your compulsive behavior makes you vulnerable and requires you to be honest with yourself. But being compulsive is even RISKIER when you use this behavior for short-term "solutions" and satisfactions! Dare to master it. It's the type of RISK that will reap you countless rewards.

$\mathcal{Y}$ ou will see substantial progress in your self-growth when you realize that you can control only yourself. To try to change or control another is an injustice to both of you. What right have you to decide how another should be or act? Each human being is free in his or her own right. You are free to make your own decisions, to experience your own joys, to learn from your own mistakes, to live your own life. No one can take these rights from you unless you allow it to be so.

If you choose to let someone control you, this places a heavy burden on that individual. In a way, you are being highly manipulative in controlling their feelings of guilt, anger or pity. Everyone needs and wants help or comfort, but no one really wants to be controlled by another.

You have an obligation to yourself to try to control or master those things for which you are solely responsible. However, there may come a point when you find yourself feeling helpless, knowing you can no longer help the situation or do anything further to remedy the problem. Realizing this frees you to be able to understand that there are also some things that are best left up to a "higher power".

You can never be in complete and absolute control of life—no matter how hard you try. Life is full of surprises and of situations that you cannot anticipate. Perhaps this is so in order for you to RISK learning more about yourself and life—one day at a time. Viewing control in this manner may be of comfort to you as there is no longer a reason to fear tomorrow or feel desperate today.

Whether you want to believe it or not, you have your own source of courage readily available whenever needed. What zaps your ability to believe this is your tendency to compare your courage with someone else's, believing that they have more than you do. You get in trouble and lose faith in yourself when you make comparisons between yourself and others. They are not you, just as you are not them! Each person is an unique individual with different life experiences. Your sources of strength, of courage, will be drawn from different places and for different reasons or times. The fact is that you **do** possess courage. It is at your disposal, to be used as needed—if you're interested and willing.

One of the hardest lessons to learn in life is having the courage to accept yourself—as you are. You should actually like and love yourself. This occurs when you take the time needed to understand yourself and to view yourself honestly. Honesty is difficult to deal with as you may very well discover parts of your inner self that you do not like. You are admitting that you are not perfect and are indeed vulnerable. But only when you've dissected your many parts and examined them one by one, can you then have the courage to RISK putting yourself back together in a way that is more comfortable and fosters your self-growth. Being more at ease allows you the courage needed to work on those negative areas for your betterment. True acceptance of self, including your imperfections, further provides you with the courage to RISK loving another person.

Finding the courage to express your heart-felt feelings is difficult. You may fear that by expressing your honesty you'll be rejected, ridiculed, misunderstood or you'll scare the other person away. Unfortunately, you immediately think of all these negative factors and **not** the fact that your honesty could lead to deeper and more meaningful relationships, true unselfish love, happiness and greater joy. Perhaps you should ask yourself what is the worst thing that could happen if you did express your feelings. Chances are, that you would feel much better about yourself as you were sharing what was important to you. The alternative is to hold these feelings inside. Even if they are sad or negative feelings, what good can come from hoarding them? You may find you run an even larger RISK of actually detesting yourself and ruining your health— all because of your fear of sharing. You need to push yourself to find the inner courage to communicate what you feel. This is tremendous RISK but one well worth taking?

You must **never** give up on yourself! Always seek your inner courage to trudge on— especially when you're discouraged. **You** have the ability to do this! Know that the hard times you are experiencing cannot last forever. They will eventually pass on, leaving you with even more courage and hope in the future.

CRITICISM

A criticizer is one who possesses a negative attitude towards life in general. They are the people who are content with nothing. They find fault with everything and everyone.

I was a severe criticizer. I truly believed and operated from the false pretence that people were basically not OK and therefore, needed all the help they could get. And of course, I had all the "right" answers and suggestions. My ways of doing things, my opinions, my ideas were always excellent. I was a very egocentric person. Yet selfishness was not part of it. I've always cared deeply for people. I wanted to perhaps be the ultimate helper— the perfect person. Quickly discovering that this was an impossibility, I chose to criticize those who tried, including myself.

I feel that those of us who tend to criticize others are using this as a cover-up for our own inner fears. Do you fear you're not "good" enough? Do you fear allowing your true feelings to be seen, heard, or felt?

It's a terribly destructive, vicious cycle. And if you feel you yourself could qualify as a criticizer, I urge you to work towards changing this trait. It is a well-worn bad habit. Habits can be changed if you choose to change them.

How many "criticizers" do you know who are truly happy people? They are unhappy with themselves. It's easy to take out your own anger on others, but in this process of relieving or taking pressure off yourself, you create more stress. Now you may also have to deal with the guilt involved in hurting others.

If they could be truly honest with themselves, they would not feel a need to hide behind their criticisms, creating a false kind of honesty. Acceptance of self is the best way to lose the habit of criticizing.

Complaining only helps to increase your dissatisfaction with life. It does nothing to help. Complaining is a waste of precious time that you could use constructively. Doing something about what you dislike takes effort and

44

courage. A criticizer elects to do nothing.

If you find that you have two sets of standards, one for yourself, and another for others, beware! Whatever "special" allowances you make for yourself should be made for others as well.

Treat others as you wish to be treated. If you criticize others, how would YOU feel if that person were you?

Remember that when you receive criticism, it is only someone's opinion. When your self-esteem is low, you tend to be more sensitive to criticisms. When you're sinking from a case of low self-esteem, just think of the good things about yourself. Do not allow the negative feelings to penetrate the barrier of good you have placed around yourself! Yes, you are indeed of worth and importance. Never doubt this! RISK accepting criticism from others with ease; RISK experiencing compassion for others.

DECISIONS

You are faced with making decisions every day—from small choices to making important changes in your life. Thus it's a process you need to feel comfortable with. When it's time to make a decision about something, you feel in your heart that it's time to make a change and take some action. Many times you may be apprehensive, unsure or scared as to what to do—but the decision still has to be made. You must make decisions where a situation or problem interferes with your ability to live life fully—where your growth is restricted. To choose otherwise, whether it's by procrastinating or letting someone else think for you, is allowing a great injustice to exist within yourself.

When considering a change, **do not** panic, rush, or act out of desperation. Decisions made under these circumstances are usually unfair or unworkable in the long run. Decisions made as a result of fleeing or avoiding an unpleasant situation will not help you either. No matter where you go, the problems will always be with you, in your mind—until you decide to do something constructive about them.

Decisions are a mixture of gut feelings, rational thinking and evaluating. You need to be patient with yourself in taking time to consider all aspects and alternatives. Try to visualize possible outcomes. Keep in mind that your fears, anger, bitterness or advice from others should **not** interfere. You should seek inner guidance and **not** that of your friends, family or work associates. No one can make decisions for you. Others can provide comfort, but to seek advice is unfair to both parties. Making your own decisions is your responsibility. Decisions made that include compasssion, tolerance and kindness towards yourself as well as others, are decisions that you can easily live with peacefully. If the burden is more than you can handle, it may help to meditate or pray—keeping your mind open for an answer.

Once important decisions are made, do not think they can be reversed easily or that you can be "wishy-washy". Wavering back and forth only hinders your positive efforts towards change and adds to your discomfort. This may also lead to an endless and useless pattern of wasted time and energy in doing nothing. Be steadfast and positive about your decision. This helps give you the strength needed to make the changes involved. Be proud of the fact that you have chosen to RISK becoming your own master in doing what is best for you!

DESPAIR

When you feel desperate, your mind is so confused that making clear, reasonable decisions is an impossible task. When you're feeling desperate, it's like looking at a total stranger and thinking, "Gee, she's/he's sort of crazy right now,"—while the other part of you goes through all the frantic motions of feeling and being desperate. When something tends to dominate all your thoughts—turning over and over in your mind—you are feeling desperate. Unfortunately, all this repetitive thinking does is to lead you down the path to deeper despair.

These are times when you tend to over-react and try to do "something" when in fact, the very best thing to do is simply nothing! When you feel desperate, you should try to literally let go of the situation. Obviously, your frantic activity and thoughts aren't solving the problem. Why not admit that you are feeling hopeless and helpless. Realize that you've done all that you know how to do, or can do about it. This is very difficult. But admitting that you are hurting and scared helps you let go of these fears that are presently dominating and controlling you.

Try to quiet your mind and really let go. Meditate. Pray. Walk. Breathe deeply. Try to collect the scattered pieces of your inner calm. When you tend to feel sorry for yourself, it would do you a world of good if you would stop, even just for a moment, and have compassion for other people. You would like to assume that you're the only one who has problems. But, remember that there will **always** be those in need of love and help who are much "worse off" than you. When you are feeling sorry for yourself, know that this is where Despair loves to dwell.

Be aware that sometimes you may have chosen to keep your desperate feelings rather than take a glimpse at Hope. Whenever you feel Hope, there is no longer a reason to feel desperate! In order to feel hopeful, you must let go of your old familiar pattern of feeling desperate! Only when you can do this, can you then attempt to do something constructive about the situation. By having hope, you become an optimist, rather than remaining a pessimist about life.

Even in those times of your life when you feel most desperate and totally hopeless, remember that there is always something to be learned or gained from any experience. This is part of life. And that for all the "bad" times there are many more "good" times. Your faith in life can be a great comforter during these 'times. **Nothing** is totally hopeless unless we believe it to be so! Why not RISK feeling hopeful?

DISCOURAGEMENT/FRUSTRATION

E veryone feels discouraged or frustrated at one time or another. This is a natural thing to feel when you are trying to do too much at once; when nothing seems to be going right for you—despite your efforts; or the whole world around you seems to be one big grouch.

Regardless of the reason you feel discouraged, it is usually the end result of being "over-loaded". You are capable of doing just so much in the way of coping with problems, changing, working, studying or just processing new information. Just as my computer balks and makes funny sounds, refusing to store additional information in its memory because the disk is full, so you similarly react. When you feel discouraged or frustrated, you are saying in effect, "Enough is enough!". At that point, your inner workings are telling you it's on over-load and it's time to quit for a while. When viewed in this way, frustration is really a healthy thing to experience as it keeps you from pushing yourself beyond your limits.

Be aware that you are only human—a being who is **not** perfect—is not Superman or Superwoman. You can do just so much each day. You can do just so many things "right". If another person is the focus of your frustration, remembering that he or she is also human and imperfect may help to ease your tension.

The key here is to always remember that tomorrow is another day, that life is a variety of ups and downs. Look forward to tomorrow as an "up" day. It's a new beginning ready and waiting for you. Do acknowledge your "down" feelings but do not give in to them. Find a short phrase of encouragement that you can repeat over and over to yourself! For example: "Chin up!" or "Hang in there!"

Many times, all that is needed is a short rest away from the frustrating factors. Take some time away to quiet your mind and temporarily let go of the problems. They're certainly not going anywhere, so why hang onto them so tightly?! Besides, what good is it going to do to carry these things around, weighing and dragging down your spirits even further?

So, what are you going to do right now—
besides feel frustrated? Why not RISK doing
something fun and allowing yourself a short
fiesta! It certainly can't hurt—most likely it
will help.

ENERGY

I t seems that personal energy—mental and physical, comes and goes as it pleases. You seem to have little or no control over it. At times you feel so terrific and full of energy that you think you could go on forever, ignoring sleep and eating only what is necessary. You attack life head-on with vigor and with a tremendous feeling and love of life.

At other times, you feel so awful that you're even exhausted when you get up in the morning. No matter how much or what you eat, or do, you don't perk up. Nothing seems to go right for you. All you see are problems and more problems. Getting up in the morning is hard and these are the types of days when you usually stub your toe in the process! Life just seems tough to live.

There are also times where one moment you feel you're on an energy high and the next moment you're past empty according to your energy gauge. You're like a yoyo being pulled up and down, up and down, yanked and stretched on the string, extended to the very end of your limits in both directions. As a result, you feel very frustrated as you don't know what to expect from yourself. You don't know when you can count on yourself to have the necessary energy to do your work or even to pursue your hobbies or fun activities. You start something and never finish it because you suddenly lack the energy to do so. Just as your energy drastically shifts, so do your moods. One minute you're Mr. Nice Guy and the next minute a real crab.

Is it true that you have no control over this whole process? No. If you are interested in grasping hold of the situation, you can, in most cases, maintain an even keel. Or, if your energy leans too far to one side, you can cope with it and right it quickly.

Energy is an interesting internal warning device housed in each of us. When your energy is extremely low, it is telling you that you're too far off center. Something needs to be corrected. It could be that you're not up to par physically and need to slow down and rest. It could be that you're not doing those things that are important to you—you're ignoring your own needs. It could be a combination of things. Whatever it is, it needs your attention. And, until you give yourself that attention, you can expect things to remain the same or to become even worse.

When you are on course, headed in the right direction according to your chosen life goals, you will have the energy needed to tackle whatever comes along. You will amaze yourself with your ability to keep going, to overcome your usual procrastination and to complete the tasks you've set out to complete.

So, if you're presently devoid of energy, what is it that is bugging you? What is it that is pushing you off course? Once you have the answers and deal with them, your energy will be restored.

If you're stuck and nothing comes to mind as to what is wrong, try to maintain a positive attitude. Realize that this is just a low time and that you'll eventually rise above it—that you won't be stuck there forever. Keep yourself in good shape by eating properly, getting daily exercise and adequate rest. Try not to feel desperate or to spend all your mental energy trying to solve this problem. Relax. Look for little things that you can enjoy and feel good about. Treat yourself with kindness.

Energy is indeed, a wonderous thing. It's something we do have control over. It can be a strong ally. RISK learning to control it and use it to your advantage!

ENTHUSIASM

When you're enthusiastic, your're gung-ho about something in life or about life itself. You are excited, energetic and full of good feelings. Things are not perfect. There are problems present and things could go wrong, but you can still maintain your optimism if enthusiasm is present.

Enthusiasm is a wondrous thing. It is contagious and spreads like wildfire easily— with a little help from yourself. As with most things in life, some effort is necessary on your part to generate enthusiasm. You must first pick it up, grasp it in your hands and then quickly plant it—lest you lose it. Like a seed planted in the ground, it grows millions of times its original size. And, if carefully tended by you, will provide an ever present crop for you to harvest.

In order to be enthusiastic you must be willing to **RISK** maintaining a positive outlook towards life. You must allow only positive seeds to be planted, culling out the negative and casting them aside. Since the negative seeds only take up valuable space in your garden and are worthless bearers.

You don't feel enthusiastic? Can't think of anything that would excite you or "turn you on"? Do you ever feel a little angry (or envious) when you observe another's enthusiastic manner? Do you feel you can't have enthusiasm or don't deserve it? Do you feel it's impossible to have because of your problems? These are ways that a **negative** person thinks. And, since you are reading about Enthusiasm, you will have to give up these negative thoughts! They're blocking your view. It's like useless weeds growing wild and out of control. You have got to put a stop to it right now!

How? Even if you don't feel enthusiastic, start **acting** that way. Why not smile at your cranky neighbor for starters? Why not look for something that's **good** about your life or about the problems you're experiencing. Why not take a rest from your negative mind? Concentrate your energy on caring or sharing with another. Do you know what will happen? You'll feel better, joyous, and more vivacious. You'll feel like you're a completely different person. And you are because you've become an enthusiastic supporter of enthusiasm. You've RISKED planting the seed. Isn't that just fantastic, super wonderful, terrific and "out of sight"?!

You have heard stories about people who seem to have a fantastically joyous and positive outlook towards life even while experiencing great tragedy. What makes these people so strong, confident and loving in the face of terrifying circumstances? What helps them continue on when most of us would have given up and quit, leaving us with only a collapsed and hopeless spirit?

Faith. Faith helps shrink your problems into manageable sizes. Not that the problem is any different, you've just changed your perspective about it. You've learned that there is just so much you can do. The rest is up to whatever powerful force placed you here on earth in the first place. Call it God, the universal spirit, a higher power or whatever you like.

The fact is, having faith can be a very wonderful healing force operating within you. It's nice to be able to rely on your spiritual "reserve" for comfort and support. It can act as your long-lost security blanket.

Some people feel that faith is a lot of rubbish. They feel that if it cannot be concretely proved, then it cannot exist. But there are many things that cannot be proven or measured in a black and white fashion—such as love or trust. You just have certain feelings about them. You know you have them but it is impossible for you to identify them to the point of proving their worth on paper. So it is with faith. It is just a special group of feelings you have.

One nice thing about faith—especially for those who doubt its existence or worth—is that it doesn't need a total commitment from you to operate. If you are willing to accept it just as a remote possibility, then it is present. It is simply a gift.

If you accept this gift, you will find your life is fuller, richer and brimming over with love. You will find it easier to accept what you cannot change and to let go when you need to do so. And, you may even feel a little bewildered or dizzy by its power to comfort you!

Believe me when I tell you it has drastically changed my own life, as I was basically a non-believer. But being skeptically open allowed me to find an inner peace that I thought only existed for gurus, nuns or priests.

Faith is out there where you are, waiting. You can identify it by the depth of your inner feeling of peacefulness. It is operating when you allow yourself to let go of that which you cannot change, knowing you've done all you can do. And whatever happens now, will be best and what needs to be, for that particular situation. Would you be willing to RISK trying to accept Faith even as a mere possibility?

FEAR

One of the best feelings you'll ever experience comes from realizing that you are loosening the grip that fear tends to hold on you. To be able to push aside your fears so that you can pursue your hopes and dreams, is a difficult thing to learn. But be assured, there are always steps you can take to help you be more comfortable in alleviating your fears. Having the courage to seek them out and recognizing their hold on you is the first step. Once you know what you're up against or facing, fears don't seem as overwhelming and frightening. Your self-confidence tends to soar when you realize YOU are the one who is master—not fear!

Everyone has their own private collection of fears: fear of the dark, the unknown, of success, of heights, of snakes, of communicating feelings, etc. You'll always be afraid of something at sometime in your life. Just know that many of our fears are unwarranted. They have no concrete basis. Therefore, does it do any good to worry about them, to be upset by them, to be obsessed by them? Look forward to life. Don't peek fearfully around the corner. Stand tall and know that YOU can deal with whatever comes in the future. If you panic and become sick with fear, how can you handle the situation to your advantage? You can't!

If you find an oil leak in your car, but choose to ignore it, your car's engine will eventually blow up. It cannot run without an adequate amount of oil. You've two choices. You can continuously add more oil or you can permanently fix the leaky engine part. Either way, time and your efforts are involved. The easier way, less (initially) costly solution may **seem** to be to continually add oil as needed. But, if you were to add up all the hours you'd spend putting oil in the car, and figured the actual cost of the oil used, you'd probably conclude it would have saved you more in the long run by fixing the engine when you first observed it leaking.

Your mind cannot run without an adequate amount of love and joy. Love and joy cannot exist where fear flourishes. Love and joy keep you mind running smoothly, helping to soothe and grease any rough parts of life you experience. Allowing fear in is like allowing a persistent leak to exist in your mind. It continually drains you of energy.

Tackle your fears one by one. Overcoming fears means leaping into freedom. RISK tackling any fear-leaks now—no matter how minute they seem, before any expensive major mind-overhauls are required!

R egardless of how you presently feel, you have the ability to give. To give of yourself to another means to listen and to be so interested in the other that you momentarily forget about yourself.

Have you ever watched someone stammer, blush or look horrified, when given a sincere compliment? A compliment is a simple gift of giving from one to another. For many, it is extremely difficult to accept such gifts from others—though they may easily be able to give them to others.

A person who is comfortable in giving is one who knows how to graciously accept these same gifts him or herself. They know that something given honestly from the heart is one of the most precious gifts you can receive.

How much do you really give to those you love—not material gifts, but heart gifts? Do you really show you care by giving of yourself in words, gestures and actions?

Part of the joy in giving is to surprise another. If you are a poor receiver, you spoil not only your chance for joy, but the other's as well. People usually stop giving because the other does not acknowledge the gifts. Yet, in genuine giving, the giver will receive joy regardless of whether their gift is acknowledged or not. Giving with no expectations in return is an extremely important life lesson to learn, yet the rewards are greater than ever imagined.

Will you RISK giving of your time, presence, or attention to someone else today? Will you take time to also be kind to yourself? If you'll take the chance to RISK giving, you'll find that what you give will be returned threefold! NEVER give up giving!

B ecause of the way life is, from time to time you will experience losing people or things that are special to you. This could involve a good friend moving away, the loss of a job, an organizational management change at work, the death of someone you've loved, the end of a love relationship, an accident that results in altering your lifestyle, the loss of your youth or physical stamina, etc.

When you feel grief, your perceptions of what is important may be altered. You feel a numbness about your entire daily world, being oblivious to life's everday trivialities. You may feel that you cannot go on and tend to deny what has happened. You hurt so badly that you are in a state of shock. You may feel fragmented with a big chunk of you suddenly gone. It's as if a vital puzzle piece has been misplaced so that the picture can't be completed. These are all natural and healthy reactions to a loss.

Whatever the loss, allow time to help ease

your pain. You need to face your pain, feel it but then be able to let go of it. Holding onto pain forever will not allow you to change or to grow. However, ignoring the pain you feel will also hinder your ability to grow.

Though unpleasant to experience, many times you can learn something from the pain of loss. Pain can help to open your mind's eyes in taking another look at life. It shows you just how delicate and wonderful life is. But also, it reminds you that your life, all life, **is** finite.

Recently, I saw someone with whom I used to work. Two days later, I read his obituary in the newspaper. Here one minute, gone— forever—the next. Yes, we are vulnerable to life, and to death. And, because of this, to choose to stay stuck in life by continually grieving a certain loss is wasteful of your life!

Acknowledge your pain and grief. Face your losses head on. See what you might learn from this experience. Regroup the pieces of your life so that a new puzzle picture is formed. And then, RISK getting on with your life!

G uilt is a gruesome method of shaming one-self. Feeling shame does nothing to improve a problem. It in fact, can make the situation even worse. Because you feel so bad, it is not possible to direct your thinking in a constructive direction. Guilt therefore obstructs your ability to change or even to grow.

Guilt exists because of your inability to forgive yourself. Regardless of whether you were at fault or sorry because of what happened, you still need to forgive yourself. You need to allow the situation to come to rest. Brooding about it does not change it. What has happened, has indeed, happened. The best thing you can do is to learn from it. The worst thing you can do is to feel guilty about it.

Guilt is a very powerful, negative force. If allowed to dwell inside you, it will rule you. How you feel, what you say or do in life will be reflected by your feelings of guilt.

If you feel a need to be perfect, chances are

that you're carrying a large load of Guilt on your shoulders. Where does it say that you must be perfect? What law states that you must berate yourself for any mistake you make? Who says that you are not allowed to have flaws? No one but yourself! A person filled with guilt is being unduly self-critical.

Some people secretly harbor their guilt for years at a time. They fear that their deeds of guilt are too awful to share with anyone. Fact is much of this guilt is quite inoffensive, and considered harmless or irrelevant to how they are viewed as individuals! It is rather, a figment of your own imagination and horror. If your are drenching wet with guilt, ask yourself, "What good am I doing by feeling this way?" As long as you harbor guilt, you cannot feel good about yourself. Others do not judge you by the amount of guilt you hold steadfast in your heart. They view you by the good they naturally observe in you.

Instead of wallowing around in the mud with guilt—getting nowhere except digging a deeper, dirtier mud hole, make a committment to yourself to clean up your act. How? Let it go. Say goodbye to it. Accept that what happened is past history. Forgive yourself. Allow yourself to be human. RISK living in the now—for today. Forget the past. Learn from your mistakes. And please, don't make others feel guilty either!

HONESTY

You have your own opinions and probably express them regularly. "If I were President, I'd....She sure is stupid doing it that way....It's ridiculous what you put up with...etc."

Talk is easy and free flowing. But talk such as this is just that. Talk does not mean action, following through on something, or commitment to something. It is idle.

If you are truly honest with yourself and others, you live what you say. You do not place any facades in front of yourself to appear "better" or "bigger" than you really are. You just are, and you RISK being just yourself.

If you have been living a life of facades, especially for a very long time, it may be that you don't have a good feel as to how you really are!

Honesty begins with self. It involves being willing to take the RISK of viewing yourself nakedly, unadorned, head on. This can be a very painful thing to experience, but the reward is being able to live your life genuinely and openly. You honestly have no reason to cover up your feelings, blemishes or "ugly, imperfect" parts. The result? Peace of mind.

You will find relief from your anger at life by viewing yourself honestly. By changing your point of view, you change your focus from blaming others to being willing to study your own actions and behavior. You are willing to try to understand what prompted your anger.

Self-honesty will make you feel good about yourself. You will also have more energy as you are no longer wasting valuable time on useless anger.

Self-honesty enables you to be open to your feelings and to trust your perceptions.

Most people operate on several levels of honesty and you'll find this true for you. What's interesting is that with the passage of time, you may find these levels will become more meaningful and deeper in scope. You may choose not to be completely honest with a loved one for fear of hurting them. Or, you may not be totally honest with another in business situations.

There are no set standards or patterns in being honest. You are the only one who can decide how you will operate—bound by your own moral convictions and beliefs.

Sometimes, even if around those people you care about, you feel a deep sense of loneliness or an emptiness. If this is so, it may be that you are cloaking your honest feelings for fear of being vulnerable or of being rejected. Know that no real sharing, caring and love can take place under false pretenses.

True friendships and love relationships must be based on a level of honesty that is comfortable for both parties. And that involves trust. Trust is letting yourself be honest with another, knowing that they will accept you—faults and all. They will not betray you.

Many people will go through life masking their honest feelings because their fear of betrayal is so strong. They do not feel they can afford to RISK honesty. The result? They restrict their ability to live fully and experience much discontentment. Can YOU really afford this? Is this what you want for yourself?

HOPE

Hope is being able to rise above your own problems—no matter how awful and hopeless they appear to be and view life compassionately. When you are open to the possibility of the fact that miracles do indeed exist, you open yourself up to possibilities you felt were non-existent.

The energy you spent viewing the problems negatively is now converted to energy spent in positive ways. If you are open to believing something is possible, even remotely, you are open to growth, to expanding, to jumping hurdles.

Part of hope is acknowledging that there will be times when you realize you've done all you can do. And, that you willingly give up your hand of control. You are effectively releasing your resistance to what in fact **is**. Regardless of what you do, whatever is, will continue to be.

Letting go of these hopeless feelings of frus-

79

tration and desperation gives you the chance to be able to replace these feelings with hope and faith. As long as you continue your "death-grip" hold of the situation, there is no chance for positive change. You have placed yourself in a no-win situation. You are torn between your deepest feelings and what is.

Keep in mind that the changes **you** want may not be always possible—or advisable. But in your willingness to accept hope, you are comfortable in accepting that whatever will be, whatever is to happen next, is for the best. This brings about a quiet presence that you know you didn't feel before. It is peace of mind and the feeling of hopefulness.

At this moment, you may be unable to view what has happened in a positive manner. If you stretch your thinking by searching for lessons to be learned from your problems, eventually you will be able to see their goodness. There is a natural flow in life and it will provide you with the comfort you need—the hope you need.

Hope provides you with an invisible comforter. When you're too tired and sad to do anymore, you know all you have to do is to pull up the covers. The RISK you must take is accepting the comforter that is offered to you. And, use it to warm your heart so that once more, you can love life as it is!

No matter your background, economic situation or how or where you live, everyone is equal. Therefore, you should never compare yourself to others. Never make personal judgments or criticisms toward others. You should instead, look for the good in all persons and humbly accept yourself and others for what you and they are. It's when you feel superior or inferior that you have lost your own humility.

Humility is keeping an open mind and learning that pride gets in the way of your growth. In order to experience humbleness, you have to be able to admit you can be wrong at times. At the same time, there is no reason to dwell on your past "failures". You are not infallible and therefore should not dwell on your expectations of how others should be. Humility is admitting that you don't know everything. There will always be much to learn—regardless of how extensive your present knowledge.

Being humble means maintaining a delicate balance of being the best you can be—without feeling superior. You are but one individual living amongst millions on earth. You are but a mere speck in this vast universe. Yet, you are a special, unique individual who is highly treasured, as is all of life! Your pulse helps the world tick along.

Being proud of our accomplishments and successes is healthy and gives us a good feeling. But to brag of your success is to inhibit your ability to feel that special oneness with the rest of mankind. A humble person enjoys sharing his victories but feels no need to brag. They enjoy people as people, as they do themselves. To lose humility is to lose a large chunk of precious life! Can you RISK that?

When you think about the word Joy, many different things come to mind. Often your joy seems dependent upon money, other people, physical diversions or activities. You tend to seek joy by going to parties, seeing movies, watching television, taking vacations, buying items you want but don't really need, etc. It seems that you are able to experience joy only under certain conditions, circumstances or times.

It's as if you collect your joys and carefully preserve them so that you can increase the number of canned goodies you have stored in your pantry of life. And every so often, you take one down and open it—perhaps trying to re-experience it, hoping to get a taste of those long ago faded feelings of joy, but it doesn't seem to help you feel joyful now.

Why? Because you can't "can" joy. It can't be preserved for your future use. It's like fresh fruit. If it is not used and enjoyed, it rots and is wasted. Of course you can preserve fruit, but it's not the same. So, if you want to enjoy fresh fruit, you must continually go to the store, buy it and use it immediately. So it is with joy. To enjoy joy, you must experience it constantly and not save it for future use.

Joy is not contingent on circumstances or certain conditions. You can afford all the joy you want and need, regardless of your financial conditions. It's a free commodity, just for the taking. It's available to you at any time, day or night, seven days a week, 365 days a year. It's habit forming and healthy for you to experience. It can make the difference between your loving or hating life. Interested in getting some joy for your very own use everyday?

There is no need to engage in a massive search, treasure hunt or complicated guessing game. All you need to do is to look at yourself. Joy begins in your heart. It's there when you get up in the morning and doesn't even end when you lay your head down to rest. It just keeps on coming to you—even in your dreams. It allows you to experience it—**if you choose.**

The true joy you seek is found in the thousands of ordinary, daily things that occur in your life: in watching the sun rising, in listening to the birds singing, in doing something well and knowing it, in observing a child playing, in walking, in hugging, in helping another, in doing what is important to you, in sharing, in being just yourself. If you would allow yourself to feel—**really** feel joy in all that you do, you would no longer feel a need to search for it. You would no longer make it contingent upon certain times of the year, certain persons or how much money you have on hand. You would not feel a need to can it and save it for special occasions, as every day, every hour and minute, are special times if joy is present. Joy is experienced by taking a different perspective in all that you do, think, say or see. Seek to discover just how many times you feel joy each day. Why not allow your present sadnesses, biases, and prejudices to be canned, sealing them in air-tight containers so they will not have the chance to leak out. Then, ceremoniously carry them to the local dump and heave them away. And, RISK feeling great Joy in doing it.

LETTING GO

L etting go is essential to **any** love relationship. You own your own freedom and have
no right to inhibit another's. You have no right
to try to control or to "fix" another human
being. Letting go involves laying down your
criticisms and judgments. You waste precious
time and energy when you concern yourself with the actions or reactions of others.
You must allow every person to live his or her
own life regardless of how you feel about it.
Letting go means being able to offer love with
no strings attached!

You have an obligation to care about and love
others. It does **not** mean however, that you
should do their "work" for them. True caring
means letting go even if you know the other
may fall flat on his face or stumble around.
Everyone has lessons to learn. Let them learn
their own lessons by and for themselves, their
own way—as you must do for yourself.

Several months ago, I was very upset about a
problem. I worried about it, agonized over it,

cried a lot and found myself very depressed by my sense of hopelessness. I could not figure a way to help myself out. No concrete solution seemed apparent to me. Feeling utterly drained emotionally and being physically sick, I decided to just stop thinking about it. I decided to give up—to surrender, admitting that I didn't know what to do. To help myself relax, I took a long walk and listened to some of my favorite music. At the end of the day, I felt surprisingly calmer. I continued my efforts to disregard the problem for several days. The next day, while taking one of my daily walks, a sensible solution suddenly came to me. I marveled at how simple and easy it was to do.

I'd still be plagued with this problem today if I had insisted on holding on to it; I'd be a "basket case." I had to admit that I didn't have all the answers. I had to admit I was too tired to continue the struggle.

Work from a rational basis—not on an emotional one. If you will allow yourself to let go of problems—to detach yourself from the situation, you will experience peace of mind. If you hurt, remember that you may, if you choose, let go of that pain. The hurt you feel, you have allowed yourself to feel and to experience. By letting go, you can then enlist the help of God, or your higher power, which can be of great comfort!

Most people fear taking the RISK of letting go. In order to let go, you have to relinquish your control. It's tough to willingly give up something that is troubling you. Let go, have faith, preserve your hope, and know that what will be, **will** be. Haven't you already spent enough time trying to work on the problem, turning it over repeatedly in your mind, and placing yourself in a frenzied state? Why not relax a little and RISK letting go? Give your mind a chance to breathe unobstructed by your inner tension. Then and only then, will you find your answers and peace of mind!

I 've tried several times in the past to put my thoughts about this word down on paper, but up to now, have been unable to express them. Obviously, this is a very hard area for me. Perhaps the expression of love has been difficult for you too.

In a book entitled "On Caring", by Milton Mayeroff, he states that a person in love is one who really lives. I've heard and read this theme over and over again in the past. When in love, somehow all seems brighter and more beautiful. Though the problems don't disappear, they seem less demanding and severe. It is a wonderful feeling to experience! Trouble is, love feelings tend not to last. And, our brief touches of love are too soon forgotten remnants of the past. It's no wonder we feel cheated the rest of the time.

One tends to equate love as only with another person. But that is a narrow perspective. What about loving ourselves, as well as our pets and flowers and life? Love is being able to give to yourself—regardless of how you feel inside at that moment. It is being willing to be open in caring about others, your world, as well as yourself.

The author, Eric Fromm pointed out that **immature love** revolves around the assumption that "I am loved, therefore I love in return." **Mature** love reverses this idea so that "I am loved because I love first." It's a universal principle that the more one gives of oneself unselfishly, the more love will be received. But what do you usually do? Sit there waiting and hoping for love to seek you out? And, when it does not come while you wait doing nothing, you feel further cheated and angry. You may even question your self worth. To assume that you have nothing to offer—and to offer nothing—is to cheat yourself out of the fullness and essence of life itself!

You must get away from making your love contingent upon a result of something or someone else's feelings. You have the right and permission to love regardless of how they feel about you at that moment.

Look back through history at great men who died by another's hand and yet showed no malice or ill will towards the very person who physically destroyed them! This is true love— true compassion and caring for mankind.

For those individuals who are in love with life, you will notice a special peacefulness and feeling of calmness that seems to radiate from their eyes, their actions, and their presence. You have the ability to experience this too.

When you say you love someone, those simple words do not make it so. It is proven by your actions of caring, touching, comforting, accepting and listening to them. It is a never-ending process and one which takes continual effort. The lover who becomes lazy in this aspect soon finds himself or herself alone.

You see countless newspaper and magazine articles about loneliness. One tends to surround oneself with material possessions. You know that they'll always be around to support and comfort you. They offer you security. BUT being inanimate objects, they cannot relieve your feelings of emptiness or loneliness. Sharing yourself with others will relieve these things—even if it is with strangers.

When you discover self-love and non-contingent love for others, you may suddenly find that your material possessions do not seem as important as before. You are instead, dealing with the nitty-gritty of life. Some of the most open and loving people I've met have little material wealth. There are others who are very wealthy, yet feel no love—just emptiness. Material wealth has little to do with love. People who possess love have learned to put their "wealth" in perspective. They are not distracted by false comforts.

Learn to rely on your gut love feelings. Do not ignore them. If you have avoided these feelings, start reaching inward and re-establishing your hold on them. Grasp love with all your might. It is perhaps your strongest ally. Love provides the reason for living. When you stay in touch with love, you stay in touch with life.

To avoid love is to live life without caring for yourself or any other. RISK love. It is essential to your very survival!

PATIENCE

Tranquility can be found through practicing the art of patience. You live in a world of instant gratification. If you don't have the money for the stereo you want to buy, you can finance it by getting instant credit. If you're hungry but don't feel like fixing a meal, you can have an instant TV dinner or frozen entree, heated in a microwave oven. With time appearing to zoom by faster and faster, your needs for instant gratification are bound to increase as you try to keep up with the dizzying pace.

As your living pace increases, there's a tendency to lose a grip on your inner controls more easily. Your temper may flare quickly, sparked by something that may not have bothered you in the past. There may be a tendency to lose your "cool" faster.

Perhaps one of the best things about the days of yesteryear was that nothing was instant. It all had to be done slowly. You traveled by horse and buggy, everything was made from scratch—whether it was dinner, a chair or that buggy for travel. Slowness necessitated and fostered patience and inner calmness. No matter how bad one might want to hurry up, one knew that it would take time and require effort. Thus, people tended to plan more. They had clear goals in mind. And, very importantly, people were more involved in the actual acquisition process.

Patience today seems to have been thrown out the window. Gone forever? Not hardly, though it requires you to search and work at it.

Instant gratification is a way of life and perhaps not a "bad" thing if put in proper perspective. But it can only satisfy your basic physical needs.

The **real** needs involving your long-term desires, dreams and emotional well-being cannot be given to you instantly. They require tranquility in order to fully blossom.

Tranquility can be obtained only through patience. So, you're caught in a Catch 22.

Patience is necessary in order to experience tranquility; but you can't have tranquility without patience. The common factor? Time.

Both require time in order to develop. It is very, very easy to get caught up in your busy schedule—to fly off the handle into an instant rage at an unsuspecting clerk or loved one. As long as you continue in this pattern of life, you will probably never experience the tranquility of patience and inner peace.

RISK changing your attitude from the rat race world to one where calmness dares to exist, in and outside yourself. Remember that nothing of **real** value or of great significance was made in just a day—be it friendship, love or great invention. RISK practicing the art of patience. Try it and I'll bet you'll like its natural calming effects, reflecting your new inner tranquility!

nothing seems to pull self-confidence down faster than being rejected by another. nothing seems to do more harm than allowing these rejection feelings to stay in your mind. If accepted by you, rejected feelings can erode your inner being to the point of utter despair. Perhaps the root of resisting the urge to RISK, is your fear of the possibility of being rejected.

Rejection is a preconceived state of being. It exists because you allow it to exist. You may think you have a right to feel down because of life experiences you've had. Maybe somebody did actually hurt your feelings by rejecting your work project. Maybe your lover did make you feel unwanted when he/she pushed you away while you tried to comfort them. Maybe something happened in childhood and you're still carrying around the scars of rejection wherever you go. Whatever the "reasons" for feeling rejection, stop right now and go beneath the experience that triggered these feelings. You cannot afford the luxury of its presence, no matter how strong the temptation to give in to it.

Could it be that you are being overly sensitive? Could it be that you have not allowed for the other person to be an imperfect human being—as you are? Could it be easier to accept feeling rejected so as not to risk being vulnerable? Think carefully. Your conclusions will affect how you accept this particular rejection situation, as well as others in your future.

Feeling rejected is an unpleasant state of being, but fearing rejection is even worse. There is no way to accurately predict when rejection might occur. Therefore, by fearing it, you create a state of near panic. It freezes you so that it prevents you from wanting to do anything.

Safe? In relative terms only. Doing nothing is, in a way, a cop-out. You're assuming that all rejection is bad and negative. But many times when you are placed in a rejection situation, you can learn much from it. If your work was not up to par, it's a way of letting you know to try harder.

Perhaps being a writer, I have felt particularly sensitive to rejection. After all, my first book was turned down over 35 times before being accepted for publication. It would have been easy for me to assume that perhaps my work was no good and to have quit submitting it to publishers.

But I learned an important lesson about rejection. Most of the time it may have nothing to do with you. It may be that your timing was off. It may be that the editor liked it but had purchased enough material for the next two years. It may not have been appropriate for their editorial scope. Whatever the reason, at least I tried and kept trying. I knew that the more times I tried the better chance I had of finally placing my work.

I knew, deep down inside me, that I had done the best job I could do and that the material would be helpful to others. I had spent nearly two years working on it so obviously I believed I had something worthwhile to give. I kept plugging along between 35 odd rejection slips and finally found a publisher who wanted and liked my work.

Regardless of how another judges me, I am still a worthwhile person. Regardless whether you agree or disagree with my ideas or thoughts, I am sharing with you from my heart. Therefore your possible negative reaction is not going to stop me from trying to give honestly of myself to others.

This is perhaps one of the most difficult life lessons I have had to learn. It is a lesson that I must remind myself of from time to time. The more in tune and sensitive you are, the more vulnerable you are. Yet, what would your life be like if you chose to RISK nothing in the way of giving of yourself to others?

Please, do not permit your feelings of rejection to rule your life. RISK being and feeling and trying life out—not wasting it!

Sometimes you may find yourself continually in an action mode. You may be excited about something or perhaps feel pressured about something. You work constantly, pushing yourself beyond reasonable limits. You pour all your energies into going as fast and as hard as you can. If this continues over an extended time, chances are you're going to find yourself sick—physically as well as mentally. You have a breaking point, as does everything in life.

In industry, many times the shop maintenance team will routinely service their machinery though there is nothing wrong with it. They have found that this "preventive" maintenance extends the life of the machinery as well as keeping down the number of severe equipment failures that might occur in the future.

If you watch those people involved in hard labor tasks such as farming or house building, you'd notice that they take at least one break in the morning and another in the afternoon in addition to their lunch hour. They know that they can maintain their needed high energy levels by periodically resting for short periods of time.

When you have more work than you know how to handle in one day's time, it is hard to stop and rest. But you should keep in mind that these brief rest periods—even if only for a few minutes, would refresh you so that you could continue to do your best.

How good is the quality of your work when you're tired? How alert are you when you have taxed yourself too far? How do you feel when your nerves are as tight as a drum?

Learning to rest is extremely important to your well-being. It provides you with time to re-group your thoughts and to re-coup your energy. But, being human, you tend to raise a suspicious eyebrow at resting when you're already overloaded and feel pushed for time to accomplish what needs to be done. If you feel this way, why not just try taking brief rest periods for a few days. Only by trying it, can you see for yourself what a positive difference it could make. If you find it helps your productivity, then incorporate it as part of your daily routine—just as you brush your teeth each day. Come on, RISK resting. Bet you, too, will be amazed at the results!

RESTLESSNESS

Ever had feelings when you just can't sit still, don't seem able to concentrate on anything and nothing seems to suit? You feel like you're walking aimlessly around with no particular direction or purpose in mind. You feel you should be doing something because you have a lot of energy but you can't figure out what it is you're supposed to do. This is restlessness. It's a very uncomfortable state to experience.

Restlessness has a very definite purpose in your life. It's clearly telling you that something is amiss—that you need to examine what you're doing with your talents, your energies, your work or your life. It's cuing you in to the fact that something is wrong and needs your attention.

When washing a load of clothes, if the tub accumulates too many clothes on one side during the spin cycle, the washer stops. It cannot continue to spin out the wash water because it is so off balance that the motor won't work. Trying to force the washer to continue will most likely ruin the motor. It sure is frustrating to go to the washer to get your clothes out only to discover it has stopped on the first spin cycle! After your initial irritation at the washer, you concentrate your energy on redistributing the load. Then you close the lid and let it continue the wash cycle. It's an inconvenience, but one that's easily corrected.

Restlessness is like the out of balance washer. It's not a serious problem and can be remedied fairly easily. You need to try to figure out what is wrong—what's out of balance. Are you not relaxing enough? Are you too keyed up because of work or family problems? Are you anxious about something you need to do tomorrow? Are you ignoring your own basic needs? Are you being just plain lazy?

Whatever it is, try to key in on what it is that's bothering you. Then re-direct your energy by doing something constructive about the situation—like re-arranging the clothes in the washing machine. The longer you remain in the state of restlessness, the more uncomfortable and frustrated you will feel. Just as your clothes will never finish being washed when the load is out of balance, so will you be unable to make any progress unless you change something or do it differently. RISK changing or working on whatever is bothering you. If you do that, you'll no longer be restless.

SELF-CONFIDENCE

If you feel up until this point in your life that you've been a loser, and therefore accept that you will always be a loser, you're operating from a false thinking mode. Losers are not born, they LEARN to be losers. Self-confidence is not a genetic trait with which you are born. It is developed slowly and is a learned process. So, you have the choice of learning to develop your self-confidence or maintaining the self-defeating patterns of a loser.

You didn't embark on your life's journey to become a loser. It just happened. But how did it happen? A sure way to accept yourself as a loser is to constantly compare yourself with other people. You observe all their strengths and good qualities and you want to be just like them.

Before you buy a product, don't you generally look for first quality workmanship and material, as well as its cost? But when it comes to designer products, we assume that because it has a high price-tag attached, it must be extra special. It amazes me that people spend thousands of dollars on Designer clothes or products. A pair of blue-jeans is a pair of blue-jeans. Yet one pair cost $15.00 and the other $46.00. The difference? You're wearing a piece of the Designer on your derriere. One is plain-pocketed, the other has a designer logo.

Is that Designer really you? Do you mean to tell me that wearing a Designer's logo affects your self-confidence? If you truly think so, I submit to you that you are not allowing yourself to **be** yourself. You're obstructing your self-confidence. You are exhibiting someone else's image—not yours. The best way to gain self-confidence is to be yourself— not some cheap imitation or copy of someone else! You have your own set of unique and fantastic qualities. These are the things you need to emphasize about yourself.

There will, unfortunately always be a market for Designer products. Why? Because people want to be accepted by others. They want to be approved by their peers. If the rest of their friends are wearing Designer jeans, then they too, must wear them—even if they can't really afford them!

Me? I don't want to be like anyone else. I want to be me. I have found it's best for me to be accepted as I am. I know that I will not gain everyone's respect. But, I also know that I will always find people with whom I can feel very comfortable—where I can be myself.

Several years ago, I attended a fancy social event. Instead of sewing a dress, I purchased a very expensive one, thinking it would help me feel better about myself. Ten minutes after arriving, I found another woman wearing the same exact outfit! To top it off, this gal was a tall, willowy blond who exhibited a tremendous air of self-confidence. How one reacts in a situation like this depends upon how strong her self-confidence is. Obviously the best thing to do would be to joke about it and compliment each other. At the time though, I felt so bad that all I wanted to do was hide. At that point in my life, my self-image was too fragile. My self-image was dependent on outer-shell qualities.

No one can make you feel lowly unless you allow their comments or reactions to bring you down. If you will allow yourself to do those things that are best for you, you will feel good about you. Your self-confidence will naturally increase. Self-confidence comes from exercising your right to be YOU. Always be proud of yourself. Treat yourself with kindness and respect. Do only those things that are consistent with how you really are.

How strong is your self-confidence? Are you willing to RISK acting, being, thinking and breathing YOU—no matter what others think, or what you perceive them to think about you? If something or someone **puts** you down, and you allow it to **get** you down, then it has conquered you twice! RISK being yourself and watch your confidence soar!

A NOTE TO READERS

People need other people. It is one of the beautiful things about having the opportunity to live on earth. Being able to exchange ideas, having someone listen to you when you're down, sharing something you're enthused about, helping another, all of these things are important.

I've been helped so many times by others—especially when I was frustrated, frightened or sad. This book is my way of giving back some of the love and comfort to others who might need it. I hope it has provided some comfort to you!

You'll notice that there are some blank pages at the end of the book. Their purpose is for you to write down your own thoughts or reminders. Perhaps you have your own set of words you'd like to think about or work on that weren't included in this book.

Lastly, I'd love to hear from you—about how you've learned to enjoy the challenges of "problems" and of RISKING. If you'd like me to reply, please enclose a self-addressed, stamped envelope.

Write to me care of:

RiskTrek, Inc.
Serenity's Edge
Rt. 1, Box 558
Thaxton, VA. 24174

Whatever you do, please, live your life fully, have fun, love and laugh a lot!

Paula J. Smith

WHO IS SHE?

Paula J. Smith, a native of Washington, D.C., has earned a Master's degree, numerous awards and is the owner of her own life. Adjectives that best describe Paula include powerful, elegant, self-driven, serious yet fun-loving and an adventurer. Her enthusiasm towards life is contagious.

She feels her willingness to take RISKS is a prominent factor in her life successes. It is her belief that God endows you and every other human being with special talents and gifts. Her goal is to spark something in YOU so that you will want to act and do something with those talents NOW!

---that's Paula!